P9-DHT-384

More BROWNIE GIRL SCOUT Try-Its

Illustrated

Girl Scouts of the U.S.A.
830 Third Avenue
New York, N.Y. 10022

NO Blue

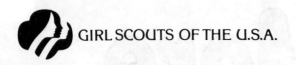

GIRL SCOUTS OF THE U.S.A.

Betty F. Pilsbury,
President
Frances Hesselbein,
National Executive Director

Credits

Director, Program	Sharon Woods Hussey
Authors	Sharon Woods Hussey
	Chris Bergerson
	Toni Eubanks
	Candace White Ciraco
	Martha Jo Dennison
	Audrey Major
	Verna Simpkins
Try-Its Designs	Chris Bergerson
Illustrator	Ethel Gold

Inquiries related to
More Brownie Girl Scout Try-Its
should be addressed to
Program,
Girl Scouts of the U.S.A.,
830 Third Avenue,
New York, N.Y. 10022.

This publication may not be reproduced,
stored in a retrieval system, or transmitted in
whole or in part or by any means, electronic
or mechanical, photocopying, recording, or
otherwise, without the prior written permission of Girl Scouts of the United States of
America, 830 Third Avenue, New York, N.Y.
10022.

©1989 by Girl Scouts of the
United States of America
All rights reserved
First Impression June 1989
Printed in the United States of America
Girl Scout Catalog No. 20-784
ISBN 0-88441-345-4

10 9 8 7 6 5 4 3 2 1

CONTENTS

Try-Its are special activities just for Brownie Girl Scouts. Your *Brownie Girl Scout Handbook* has 15 Try-Its and helpful advice on how to have fun with them. This book has 20 more Try-Its for you. Many of these Try-Its are a little harder than the ones in the *Brownie Girl Scout Handbook*, so you may have fun working on them as an *older* Brownie Girl Scout. There are four new Try-Its in each of the five worlds of interest. For each type of Try-It, you have six activities to choose from. When you have done four activities in one Try-It, you will be able to get a patch for that Try-It. You may wear this patch on your Brownie Girl Scout sash.

Some of the Try-Its have a "More to Try" section. This section is *extra* and should be done if you are really interested in the topic and want to explore it. It is not *required* to be done as part of an activity.

For many of the activities you will need to use your *Brownie Girl Scout Handbook*, so be sure to have it ready. Enjoy yourself and don't forget, "We learn by Trying It!"

MANNERS

We see all kinds of people every day. Some are old, some are young. Some have titles like "Doctor" or "Reverend." Some people you know very well. Others may be strangers. It is important to practice good manners when you talk to or interact with other people. Manners are ways of behaving that show you are considerate and respectful of others. These activities are fun ways to learn good manners.

TABLE MANNERS   You have probably been told since you were little the correct way to behave at the table. This activity will help you and your friends use these skills in a restaurant. You will need sample menus from a restaurant in your community, plates and cups, and knives, forks, and spoons. Each person should have a table setting.

Pretend you are at a restaurant. Choose one person to be a waitress and the others to be customers. Be sure to change roles.

1

Pretend to be a waitress

1. Set the table, as shown.
2. Your waitress will seat you and give each person a menu.
3. Read your menu and choose a full-course meal, including something to drink and dessert.
4. Politely place your order when the waitress asks for it. "I'll have . . . ." She pretends to write it down.
5. Wait to be served. Be sure to thank the waitress when she brings the food.
6. After you have eaten, say, "May I have the check, please?"
7. Be sure to leave a tip on the table for the waitress.

More to try: Visit a restaurant with your family and friends.

RESPECT FOR OTHERS   Showing respect for others is treating them the way you want to be treated. Your words and actions tell others whether you respect them or not. This activity will help you learn about showing respect for others.

1. Read about the Girl Scout Law on pages 7–11 of your *Brownie Girl Scout Handbook*. What guidelines does it include for showing respect to others?
2. Role-play with friends what to do if someone:

   - grabs your favorite toy
   - cuts in front of you in a line
   - does something nice for you
   - makes fun of your friends
   - looks different from you
   - beats you at a game

Do last in circle

3. Discuss how it feels when respect is shown to you and when it is not shown to you.
4. Discuss with others why it is important to show respect for your elders, including those in authority.

HAPPY HELPER   Good manners can mean helping at home. Think of a job you could do that an adult does now. It might be picking up dirty clothes or clearing the table or sweeping the floor. Offer to do the job for one week. Have you helped someone else? Is this something you could continue to do for yourself? If so, make this job your responsibility.

MEETING PEOPLE   Good manners includes knowing how to introduce yourself and others. Introductions bring people together who do not know each other. When you meet someone, relax and just be yourself. Think of meeting someone as the first step to making a new friend.

Try the following activity on introductions at home and outside the home.

1 Practice introducing yourself to others in your troop, at home, and in school. Include a smile, a handshake, and a friendly hello.

2 Practice introducing other people. Introductions are made in a certain order. The common rule is that you say a woman's and older person's names first as well as the names of people with important positions or titles. For example, you would say, "Ms. Lewis, I'd like you to meet Alexis Smith. Alexis, this is Ms. Lewis." The following list contains ideas for practicing introductions:

- a new girl in your troop
- a friend to a parent
- a girl to a boy
- a person with a special title or degree, such as father, rabbi, doctor, or judge. Try using a person's job title—for example, "Hello, Dr. Jones, I am. . . ."

3 Practice greetings used in different parts of the world. Include the following:

- In Japan, a bow is a traditional greeting. Try to bow as low and for as long as the other person.
- In Chile, a handshake and a kiss to the right cheek are customary.
- In Fiji, a smile and an upward movement of the eyebrows are how people greet one another.

More to try: Learn titles that are used in other languages and cultures. For example, "Senora" is the Spanish title for a married woman. In Japan, "San" is used after someone's name to show respect for the person.

PARTIES Being a party hostess can be great fun, but a party will be even more fun if you plan it carefully. Being a guest at a party can also be a lot of fun, and a host or hostess will love having you if you are considerate. Try this activity and you will learn a lot about being a good hostess and guest.

1 See section three on page 69 in the handbook, "Decide What You Want to Do as a Group."

2 Have a make-believe party for a group of friends. Take turns practicing being a hostess, and include:
- setting the table
- serving your guests
- saying "Thank you" and "You're welcome" to your guests

Take turns practicing being a good guest, and include:
- cheering others on at game time
- waiting your turn at mealtime and game time
- listening and responding to others
- offering assistance to your hostess or host
- saying "Thank you" when you leave

More to try: Write a thank-you note to your hostess or host.

PHONE FUN   Courtesy is important in talking to people face-to-face. It is just as important when talking on the telephone. A telephone is a very important tool. It helps people share, keeps loved ones in touch, and can even save a life. Do you know the right way to use a telephone? Can you take an important message? Do you speak clearly so the other person on the phone can understand you?

Try this activity to practice telephone know-how. With a friend, act out some of these ideas. One person can place the call and the other can answer it. Someone in the house needs help, or someone from your mother's or father's place of work calls and leaves a message, or an aunt calls to talk to you.

1 Show the wrong way to answer the phone—for example, by yelling or chewing gum in the caller's ear.
2 Show the right way to answer the phone. For example, say "Hello? Who, may I ask, is calling?"
3 Think of some other situations, such as calling a doctor, the police, or the fire department.

More to try: Have the troop decide what made each phone call good or bad.

CARING AND SHARING

You are a special person. There is no one in the world exactly like you. Your friends are special, too! You can share secrets, play, and have good times together. Your friends can help you feel good about who you are. You can do the same for them. Together, you can discover the good things about one another. These activities will help you show you care about yourself and others.

I AM SPECIAL Read pages 47–51 from the chapter "About Myself" in the *Brownie Girl Scout Handbook*. Make a chart like the one on page 48. List your favorite things. Do the activities on page 51.

do

~~PUPPETS~~ You and your Brownie Girl Scout friends can make puppets of yourselves by following the directions in the "Puppets, Dolls, and Plays" Try-It in your *Brownie Girl Scout Handbook*. Get together and pretend these puppets are friends and act out situations like the following with them:

act out (instead of puppets)

- Your best friend is crying, and you want to show you care.
- It is a troop member's birthday.
- You want to tell someone about your new bike.
- A neighbor falls and breaks her leg.
- Your friend is worried she will fail a test.
- Your friend forgot her lunch.

As a group, discuss what makes a person a good friend. What can you do to be a good friend to another person?

FEELINGS The way you feel about yourself may have an effect on the way others feel about you. Give some thought to how you feel about yourself and what others think of you in this activity. You'll need construction paper, scissors, and markers or crayons.

do

1 Fold at least five pieces of construction paper in half.

2 Write these incomplete sentences on the front of the folded construction paper:

- My friends think I am . . .
- My Girl Scout leader thinks I am . . .
- My parent (or parents) thinks I am . . .
- My teacher thinks I am . . .
- I think I am . . .

3 Open the construction paper and complete the sentence on the inside.

A FRIENDS' SCRAPBOOK Make a scrapbook that tells about your friends. Include the friends who are important to you. You will need construction paper, writing paper, a stapler, markers or crayons, and a pencil.

1 Make a cover out of construction paper.
2 Decide on the number of friends you want to include and have a page for each of them.
3 Staple the pages and cover together on one side of the scrapbook.

fold   staple   decorate

4 Decorate the cover.
5 Fill a page with good things about each friend—for example, the things she enjoys doing, things she is good at, her favorite color or game. Include her autograph, photo, phone number, and address.
6 Share your scrapbook with these special friends. Let them know how important they are to you.

from your secret pal

I CARE Be a "secret pal" to someone. Think of nice things you can do for your secret pal—for example, write a poem, make a friendship pin, send a card, or be a helper. Think of ideas of your own to use.

DIFFERENCES ARE OK Many people look different from you. Some have skin or hair that is another color. Some are taller or shorter. One person may see better and another not hear as well. All these people have the same feelings on the inside. They also have talents to share.

With your Girl Scout group, find out about ways that you are different from each other. Choose a partner and stand or sit facing her. Write down three ways your partner is different from you.

Write down three ways you are the same. Change partners and do the same thing. Come together as a group and talk about some of the ways you are different and the same. Are these differences important?

GOOD FOOD

You may know that you need to eat from four food groups. These groups are as follows:

1 fruits and vegetables
2 grain foods like wheat, corn, rice, and oats, which are used to make cereals and breads
3 protein foods like meat, poultry, fish, and eggs
4 milk product foods such as milk and foods made from milk, like cheese and yogurt.

To have a healthy, balanced diet, you should try different foods from each group. Find out more about nutrition by trying these activities.

SUGAR AND SALT   Labels list the ingredients in a food product, from the largest to the smallest amounts. Cut out or remove lists of ingredients from cereal cartons, cake-mix boxes, and frozen and canned foods. Many times, sugar or salt is added as a flavoring in food. But too much sugar or salt is not good for you. Check the labels to see if sugar or salt is at the top of the list of ingredients. If so, this product contains a lot of sugar or salt. Sugar may be listed as corn syrup, sucrose, glucose, or fructose. Salt may be listed as sodium. Try to find three labels with little sugar or salt. Make it a habit to eat less of foods containing sugars or salt.

More to try: Go with an adult to a grocery store and try to find three cereals with little or no sugar. If possible, buy and try one of them. You can use fruit to make it sweeter if it doesn't taste sweet enough for you.

GREAT GROCERIES   By now, you know some ways to eat healthier foods. You are ready to help your family make up a grocery list. Write down foods your family likes to eat during the week. Give the list to the person who does the food shopping in your home. Go with her or him to the grocery store to help choose good foods.

WHERE'S THE FAT? You may have heard bad things about fat. Everyone needs some fats every day. Fats release energy fast for your body. You find fats in plant and animal foods. Plant fats are usually oils like those in olives, peanuts, and corn. Animal fats are found in butter, egg yolks, cream, and meats.

The problems start when you eat too much fat. You can find out if there is fat in the foods you eat. You will need a large piece of paper, a pencil, hamburger meat, peanut butter, cheese, an apple, lettuce, potato chips, ice cream, or any of your favorite foods.

1 Rub a little of each food on the paper.
2 Write the name of each food under the spot you rubbed.
3 Hold the paper up to a light.
4 If you see greasy spots, the food has fat.

LUNCH All the foods we eat come from four basic food groups as mentioned on page 10. If you eat some from each group every day, you will have a balanced diet. Try this activity and learn about making a healthy meal. You will need old magazines, scissors, and one paper bag for each group.

1 Learn about the four basic food groups on pages 57–60 in your handbook.
2 In groups of two and three, cut out of a magazine pictures of foods to put in your lunch bag. (Each group should have a paper bag.) Be sure that the lunch your group makes has something from each of the four food groups.

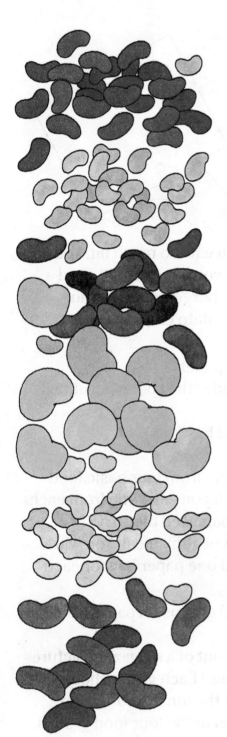

3 Explain to others what you put in your lunch bag and why.

More to try: Make a menu from the foods you put in your lunch bag. Then try the same activity for dinner and breakfast.

MILK   In our country, things made with milk usually come from cows. If you visit other countries, you will find that children drink milk from other animals. For example, children in India may drink buffalo milk and children in Lapland may drink reindeer milk. Goat milk is popular in many countries. Try this activity on milk from around the world.

1 Learn what animals give milk to people around the world.
2 Make a poster that shows all of these animals together on a farm.
3 Some people are allergic to animal milk. Instead they drink milk from soybeans, a plant. Try some soy milk or soy ice cream.

More to try: Cheese is also part of the milk family and makes a nutritious snack. Bring several types of cheese to a Girl Scout meeting and have a taste test.

PROTEINS   Protein helps your body while you are growing. Along with good exercise, it helps you develop strong, healthy muscles. Protein is found in meat, cheese, peanuts, and even beans. Learn more about protein in beans.

1 Bring in samples of dry beans.
2 Find three recipes for cooked dry beans.
3 In your troop or with an adult at home, make a bean recipe.

SAFETY

Every Girl Scout knows the motto "Be Prepared." Being prepared is really important when emergencies and accidents happen. Try the following activities and become a "Safety Wise" Brownie Girl Scout in your home, school, and neighborhood. They will help you "Be Prepared" when you are alone or when there is an emergency.

SUZY SAFETY SAYS   Can you find all the Suzy Safety pictures in your *Brownie Girl Scout Handbook*? Suzy Safety is asking you to do things the safe way. Learn the safety rules on pages 97–104 of the handbook.

Make a Safety Card game. You will need scissors, paste, and 15–20 unruled index cards. Follow these directions:

1 Cut 15–20 pictures out of magazines that show safety messages—for example, buckle-your-seat-belt pictures and don't-smoke pictures.

2 Paste each picture on an index card.
3 Mix all the cards up.
4 Place the cards on a flat area with the safety-message pictures turned face down.
5 Each player takes turns picking a card and identifying the safety message. If she is correct, the player keeps the card. If she is wrong, the next player has a chance to guess.
6 The game continues until all the cards are identified.

13

SAFETY CENTER Adults have special places where they keep important papers, phone numbers, and dates. Why can't you too have a place to keep things that will be helpful in an emergency?

Here's a way to make a safety center. You will need a hanger, a large piece of fabric, scissors, a stapler or needle and thread, markers, and at least four legal-sized envelopes.

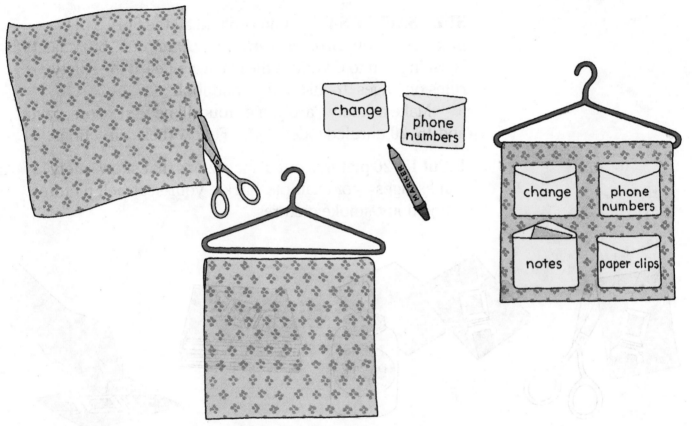

1 Cut the fabric into a large square.
2 Wrap one end of the fabric around a hanger and staple or sew with a needle and thread as shown.
3 With a marker, label the envelopes. A few ideas are:
   - Small Change
   - Emergency Phone Numbers
   - Reminder Notes

   Include an envelope in which to keep paper and a pencil for taking messages.
4 Staple or sew each envelope to the fabric as shown. Have someone hang it near the phone for you to reach easily.

STREET SAFETY   Being safe on the street is just as important as keeping yourself safe at home. To be safe on the street, you should get to know your neighborhood. Try these two activities to learn more about your neighborhood.

Take a walk through your neighborhood with an adult you trust. Look for street names, the firehouse, and the police station. Look at the people around you.

Draw a picture of your neighborhood and include some of the people, places, and things you saw during your walk. Include things from the list below:

- Where you live
- Where your troop meets
- Street signs near your home
- Favorite places you play
- Favorite stores you go to
- Parks and playgrounds in your neighborhood
- Safe places like police stations and firehouses

- A "safety haven" if your neighborhood sponsors an after-school safety-haven program

More to try: Color the safe places with your favorite color.

FIRE SAFETY   Read the section on fire safety on pages 102–104. Find out about the fire escape plan for your Brownie Girl Scout meeting place and practice it.

More to try: A fire escape plan is important, but it is not the only part of fire safety. A fire can start at night or during the day, and being alert to the danger is the first step to help get you and your family out alive. Try this fire safety activity.

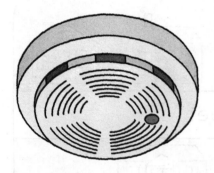

1   Learn what a smoke alarm is and how it works. If there is no smoke alarm in your home, go with an adult in your family to a hardware store and have an employee explain why smoke alarms are necessary in everyone's home.
2   Have an adult test the smoke alarm so you can hear what it sounds like.

FIRST AID   Sometimes you may be the only one around when somebody needs help. Learn a skill that could save a life in an emergency. One skill that is good to know is how to save a person who is choking. Many people do choke while eating. You can tell if a person is in trouble if she can't talk, she points to her mouth, or is turning blue. With an adult, try this exercise on first aid for choking.

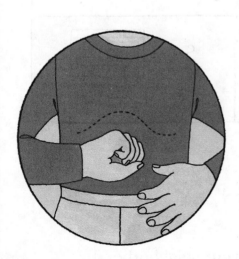

1   To find your rib cage, use your left hand, make a fist, and place it over your belly button. Then, using your right hand, make a fist and place it on top of your left fist. This spot is just below the rib cage and is important to find when you are doing first aid on a person who is choking.
2   With a partner, practice the following, **but be sure when you're just practicing not to push hard on the person's stomach**:
- Pretend your partner is choking. Keep her calm. Ask her to cough.

If she cannot breathe, cough, or speak:

- Stand behind her.
- Using your left hand, make a fist and place it over her belly button.
- Using your right hand, make a fist and place it on top of the left fist.
- Remove your left hand. Then cover your right fist with your left hand.
- Then push your fist in and up quickly.
- Keep doing this until she can cough, breathe, or speak.

More to try: Practice first aid for choking on yourself so that you can help yourself if no one is there to help you. See the pictures below.

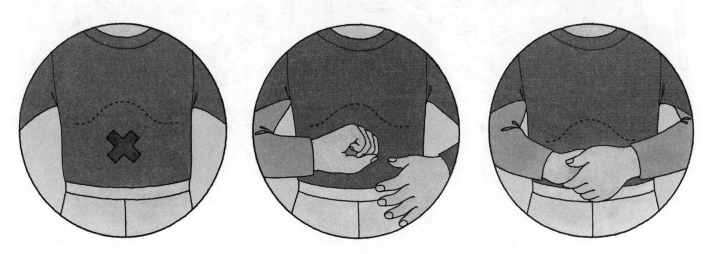

PLAYGROUND SAFETY   A playground should be a place where you can enjoy good, healthy fun and exercise. But playground equipment, if not used correctly, can be dangerous. Learn the rules of playground safety and share them with others before you have an accident.

1 Learn the play area safety rules on page 100 of your *Brownie Girl Scout Handbook*.
2 Think of some more rules for playground safety, then make and put up safety posters in your playground and at your troop meeting place.

3 Look at the equipment in the playground at your school or in your neighborhood. With an adult, give the equipment a safety check. Are the swings anchored properly? Is the slide stable? Make notes on unsafe equipment and show them to the proper officials.

IT'S A SMALL WORLD

Our world is a large world and many people live in it. In the United States of America, people who are Irish, Chinese, West Indian, French, and from other ethnic groups often live in the same community. How exciting it is to learn about our global neighbors at home or in other countries.

LOOK AT THE WORLD   Here's a fun way to learn about the world.

1   Find the United States of America on a map or on a globe. Put your finger on it.

2   Look at the other countries on the map or globe. Name two countries close to the United States and two countries far away.

19

3 The equator is an imaginary line around the world that is an equal distance from the North Pole and the South Pole. The countries farthest from the equator have a very cold climate. Find the equator and follow it around the world on a map or on a globe.

4 Name ten countries that you think have a hot climate.

5 Name ten countries that you think have cold climates.

More to try: On a map that has not been colored in, color in the continents and bodies of water. There are seven continents. If possible, use a different color for each of the continents. For example:

North America—Green

South America—Yellow

Europe—Red

Africa—Orange

Asia—Gray

Australia—Pink

Antarctica—Purple

A TREAT FROM THE FIJI ISLANDS Find Fiji on a map or globe. It is a small group of islands in the South Pacific. Notice that Fiji is just a little south of the equator, so the climate is hot. Coconut trees grow there. The coconut tree is used for shelter, food, and even clothing in some parts of the world. Try this favorite coconut treat from the Fiji Islands.

Ingredients:

    1 large banana

    1 cup grated coconut (from the baking section of the grocery store)

    3 tablespoons honey

What to do:

1 Slice the banana into many pieces and separate the pieces into three groups.

2 Put one group of the banana slices in the bottom of a bowl.

3 Pour one tablespoon of honey over the banana pieces. Sprinkle $\frac{1}{3}$ cup of grated coconut on the honey.

4 Add the second layer of bananas and pour more honey and sprinkle more grated coconut. Repeat this step until all the ingredients are in the bowl and ready to eat. Enjoy!

SCRAPBOOK   Make a global family scrapbook of children, men, and women from all over the world. Collect pictures of people from different countries from old magazines and newspapers. Your public library may give you old magazines.

1 Cut out your pictures and glue them on sheets of plain paper.

2 Cut out words you know and match them to the pictures.

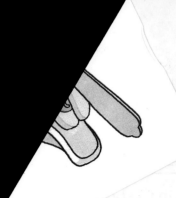

3 Make a special cover out of construction paper or cardboard.

4 Punch two holes in the cover and each page and tie all the pages and the cover together with ribbon or string.

5 Add pages to your scrapbook when you want your global family to grow.

CHILDREN'S BOOKS   Many children's storybooks have been written about families from different countries. Visit a public library and ask the librarian to help you find a story about a family from another country or an ethnic group in your country. Read the story to a younger child (maybe a brother or sister), or have someone read it to you.

WOODEN SPOON DOLL FROM YUGOSLAVIA   Imagine going to a school where toy making is a subject as important as reading and writing! Find Yugoslavia on a map or on a globe. In Yugoslavia, all children in grades one to four are taught how to make their own toys. This wooden spoon doll is a favorite.

1 Choose a wooden spoon the size you would like your doll to be.
2 Paint a face in the center of the spoon. If you prefer, you can glue on scraps of felt for the ears and nose, and sequins or small buttons for the eyes.
3 Use string or yarn for hair. Attach it to the spoon with white glue.
4 Cover the handle with colored cloth or felt. Use sequins, lace, ribbons, or buttons for decoration.
5 Fold a small square of cloth diagonally to make a woman's scarf.

TAPATAN   In countries all over the world, children play a game much like our tic-tac-toe. The game has other names. In England it is called Noughts and Crosses; in Sweden it is Tripp Trapp Trull; in Austria it is Ecke Necke Stecke; and in the Philippines it is called Tapatan. Like tic-tac-toe, the object is always to get "three in a row." Have fun playing Tapatan.

Each player needs three moving pieces. They can be pebbles, buttons, or checkers.

23

1 Draw this diagram on paper or cardboard:
2 The game is played on the nine points where the lines meet. Players take turns putting their pieces on an empty point. This continues until all three pieces of each player are placed on the game board.
3 Player one moves one piece along a line to the next empty point. The pieces can be moved up or down or diagonally. Jumping over the pieces is not allowed. Player two does the same and they continue to take turns.

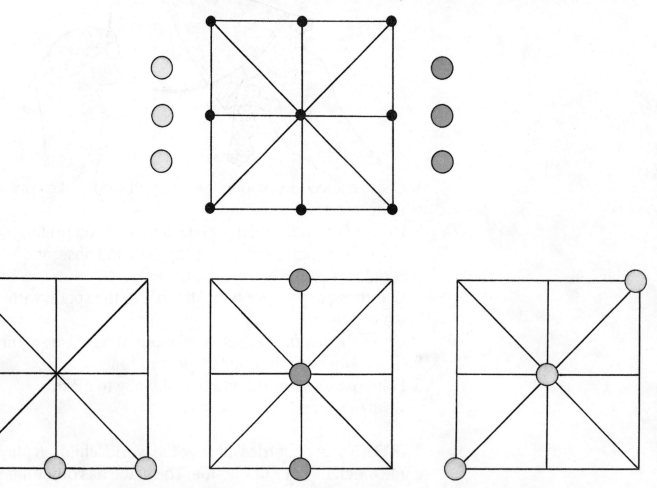

To win, a player must make a row of three across, up and down, or diagonally. If neither player can get three in a row, the game is called a draw.

CAREERS

Today, girls can look forward to many more career choices than ever before. Have you thought about what you would like to do when you grow up? Perhaps now is the time to start thinking about the future.

AUTOBIOGRAPHY   Do the autobiography activity on page 44 of your *Brownie Girl Scout Handbook*. Write about your special interests, the important events in your life, and your hopes and desires for the future. Draw or find pictures that show what you want to be when you grow up.

CAREER WORD SEARCH   Ten career-related words are hidden in the square below. See how many you can find. The words may be spelled from left to right, right to left, up or down, or on a diagonal. When you find the word, circle its letters. The first word has been circled for you. (Note: Some words share the same letters.)

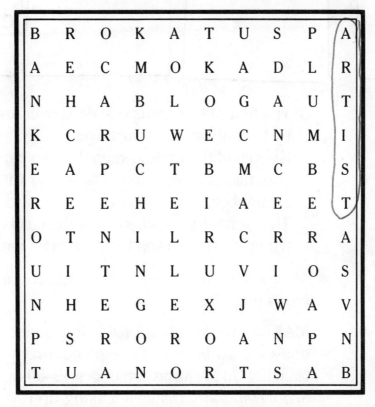

B	R	O	K	A	T	U	S	P	A
A	E	C	M	O	K	A	D	L	R
N	H	A	B	L	O	G	A	U	T
K	C	R	U	W	E	C	N	M	I
E	A	P	C	T	B	M	C	B	S
R	E	E	H	E	I	A	E	E	T
O	T	N	I	L	R	C	R	R	A
U	I	T	N	L	U	V	I	O	S
N	H	E	G	E	X	J	W	A	V
P	S	R	O	R	O	A	N	P	N
T	U	A	N	O	R	T	S	A	B

Artist
Astronaut
Banker
Beautician
Carpenter
Cook
Dancer
Plumber
Teacher
Teller

More to try: Make up a crossword puzzle or another word game using these career names or others.

CAREER CONCENTRATION With a list of about 12 careers, make a concentration game.

1 Write the name of each career on two index cards. You will have 24 cards if you have 12 careers.
2 Scramble all 24 cards together and lay them on the floor face down so that you can't read the career.

3 The first player turns one card over and tries to match it by turning another card over.
4 If you find the match, keep the two cards and try again. If you miss, the next player takes her turn. Concentrate on remembering where each career card is located.
5 The game is won when all of the cards are matched. The winner is the person with the most cards.

More to try: To make the game harder, add more career cards to it.

MAKING UP YOUR MIND Making decisions and setting goals are skills that will help you throughout your life. Read "Making Up My Mind" on pages 49–50 in your *Brownie Girl Scout Handbook*. Make a making-up-my-mind chart about two careers for you.

WORKPLACES Take a guided tour of a workplace—for example, a factory, a publishing company, a bakery, a telephone company, a department store, or a small business. Learn the types of jobs needed to make a finished product or to operate a business smoothly.

DRESS FOR THE JOB When you have a job, it is important that you wear the right clothes. Just as you wouldn't wear blue jeans to a wedding, a teller wouldn't wear shorts to her job in a bank. Decide what clothing and shoes each of the following people would wear to work.

talk about dressing properly

27

Draw a picture of each outfit, or cut out a picture from a fashion magazine. Paste the clothing to a poster board and put a career label on it.

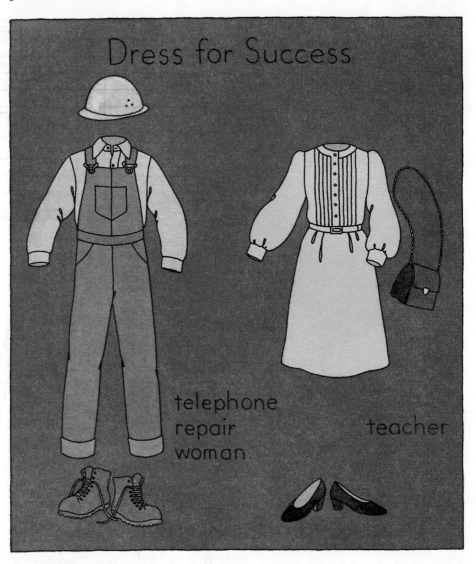

telephone repair woman	gardener
doctor	beautician
businesswoman	lawyer
teacher	mechanic

More to try: Make career-woman paper dolls. Draw outfits for them or cut outfits out of magazines to fit on them.

LISTENING TO THE PAST

Everybody has a story to tell, a story about her family, her special interests, and her life in general. When you listen to someone talk about her or his life, you are participating in oral history. This history may never be written down, but it can be passed down from one generation of family members to the next. There are many stories waiting to be discovered!

LISTEN TO THE STORIES   Ask older relatives or neighbors to tell you the stories of their lives. If possible, use a tape recorder to tape their stories. Have a written set of questions to start the conversation and to keep it going.

1 Did you have a big family? How did you get along with your brothers and sisters?
2 Was there anything your parents wouldn't let you do, or made you do that you didn't like?
3 Describe a family meal when you were a child. Do you have a favorite recipe you would like to share?
4 Describe your school. What did you study? What books did you read?

5 What games did you play as a child? What kinds of parties did you have?

6 Describe a special event in your childhood.

Add your own questions to this list. Share these stories with others.

OR

Ask family members and friends, both young and old, to tell you a funny story. Make a booklet and record these stories. Illustrate each one.

OR

Make up a skit or pantomime one or more of these funny stories.

COMMUNITY STORIES   Get to know some of the oldest people in your community. Ask them to tell you stories about the community. You may want to adopt a grandparent. (See page 79 in the *Brownie Girl Scout Handbook*.)

COMMUNITY MONTAGE   Visit buildings and historic sites in your community or in a nearby town. Take photographs or draw pictures of the areas. Make a montage. (See the montage activity on page 78 in the *Brownie Girl Scout Handbook*.)

KNOW YOUR TOWN   Visit an old cemetery in your area. Do the following activities:

1 Look for and write down the oldest dates on the tombstones of those who are buried in the cemetery. How old were these people when they died?
2 Notice the most unusual names.
3 Take pictures of the most unusual tombstones.

OR

Most cities or towns have rivers, bridges, parks, streets, schools, hospitals, and other buildings named after individual people, Indian tribes, or even trees and plants that grew in the region. Learn something about these names and their importance to your region. You can try your local library for helpful information.

BECOME A STORYTELLER   Select three stories and tell them to others in a storytelling hour, or act out the stories.

GAMES OF YESTERYEAR   Learn a game that your older relatives played when they were children. Hopscotch, paddleball, and stickball are some old favorites. Here is one game for you to try. Jacks is a "pickup" game. If you can't get a ball and jacks, you can use a small ball that fits in the palm of your hand, and ten small shells, pebbles, or beans for the jacks. The object is to pick the jacks up on one bounce of the ball, catching the ball before it hits the floor a second time. It takes time to master this game, but you can have fun trying.

1 Sit on the floor. Hold all ten jacks in your hand and toss them on the floor. They must stay where they land.
2 Toss the ball up in the air. Pick up one jack without touching any others. Catch the ball after it bounces on the floor one time (you still have the one jack in your hand).

3 If you touch another jack or miss the ball, you lose your turn.

4 After you have picked up all ten jacks, one by one, you toss all of the jacks out again and now pick up two jacks at a time.

5 The game continues. You go on to pick up three jacks at a time, then four and five up to all ten at a time.

6 The winner is the first person to pick up all ten at a time.

HER STORY

An issue is a subject or topic that people have strong feelings about and discuss. Education, health, and employment are important issues that concern women. You can learn about these issues and some others. The first activity is a requirement for receiving the patch.

TALK TO WOMEN   Ask at least three women of different ages (teenagers through the elderly) what they think are the five most important issues facing women today. Include at least two women from a race or ethnic group different from your own. Tell others what you learned from the women.

CREATE TALES   Create modern-day endings for some of your favorite fairy tales such as:

"Snow White"   "Rumpelstiltskin"

"Cinderella"   "Hansel and Gretel"

"Beauty and the Beast"   "Little Red Riding Hood"

What did the heroines in your stories do with their lives? What problems did they have? what successes? How do your endings differ from the original ones? You may create new characters and role-play one or more of the stories.

This is a list of possible things a heroine could do with her life:

- go to college
- get a job
- get married and raise a family
- move to another city or country
- become a reporter
- discover a cure for cancer
- work to send her younger sister to college
- learn how to fly a plane
- lose her inheritance and become poor
- head a worldwide peace movement
- invent something important
- save somebody's life

More to try: Read fairy tales or legends from different countries. What happens to the heroines? Are these stories different from the fairy tales you know? If so, how?

HELP IN YOUR COMMUNITY   Do one of the suggested community service projects on page 79 of your *Brownie Girl Scout Handbook*, or select one of your choice.

JULIETTE'S STORY   Read about Juliette Gordon Low's story on pages 23–25 in the *Brownie Girl Scout Handbook*. Do the blue triangle activities in the story.

More to try: Do the pink diamond activities in the story.

A HER STORY CEREMONY   Plan a simple ceremony to honor all women. Recite poems written by girls or women, perform a skit, or make up a song about a heroic woman in history, literature, or in your community. Some girls can work on the melody using piano, recorder, guitar, or any other instrument. You can invite a senior citizen to visit your troop or group and talk about her life experiences.

Prepare a worksheet like this one to plan your ceremony:

Name of ceremony _____

Date _____ Time _____

Place _____

Who will attend? _____

How will the ceremony begin? _____

What songs, poems, or skits will be included? _____

How will the ceremony end? _____

Who will bring the props, refreshments, and other equipment? _____

When will there be a practice? _____

YOUR STORY You have your own history. You have lived, have done lots of things, met lots of people. Your story will develop each day of your life. Do a time line like the one on page 63 of the *Brownie Girl Scout Handbook*. Put on your time line whatever is important to you.

My Time Line

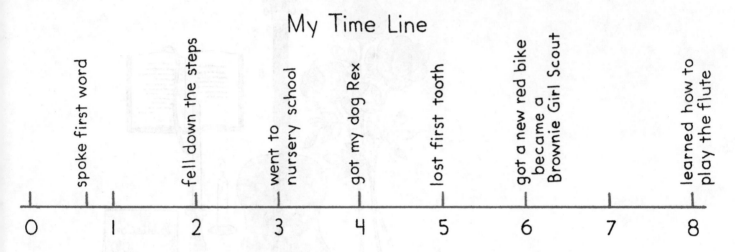

spoke first word

fell down the steps

went to nursery school

got my dog Rex

lost first tooth

got a new red bike

became a Brownie Girl Scout

learned how to play the flute

0   1   2   3   4   5   6   7   8

SPACE EXPLORER

Learning about what you see in the sky can be fun. It may be your first step in exploring space. Wondering and learning about the sun, moon, stars, and planets is something people have been doing since they first looked up at the sky. Today scientists, astronomers, and astronauts use telescopes, satellites, spaceships, and other scientific equipment to study space.

SHADOW TIME   If you have noticed that during the course of the day the sun can be seen in different places in the sky, you have noticed that the earth rotates—it spins around much like a top. And as it spins, places on earth pass by the sun. Even though it looks like the sun is moving, we are moving.

Try this activity with shadows to mark the earth's movement on a sunny day:

1 Take a stick or stake and put it in the ground. Notice that it casts a shadow. Find the very end of the shadow and mark it with another stick or a rock.
2 Leave your markers in the ground and return in an hour. Has something changed? Mark where your stick's shadow is now. Do this once more in another hour. In what direction did your shadow move? Did the stick move? What do you think moved to make your shadow move?

More to try: Keep track of the shadow's movement over a period of hours. Is there a way you could use this movement to tell time? Visit a sundial in a park or learn how to make one to tell time. Learn how to find which way is north by where the sun is in the sky.

SPACE SLEUTH   Visit a museum or a planetarium that has an exhibit or program on space or the stars. If there are none in your community, visit a library to find books on stars and space. Share something you have learned with another person.

OR

Make a model rocket. You can make a very simple rocket that will give you an understanding of rockets that are used to explore space. You will need a bottle with a cork that fits in the opening, seltzer or club soda and baking soda, paper, paint, glue, tape, and scissors.

1 Use the paper, paints, glue, tape, and scissors to add to your cork so that it looks like a rocket. (See the picture.) Make certain to leave some space at the bottom so the cork will fit into the bottle.
2 When your rocket cork is ready, take your bottle, soda, and baking soda to a clear area outside.
3 Fill the bottle halfway with seltzer. Then add two tablespoons of baking soda.

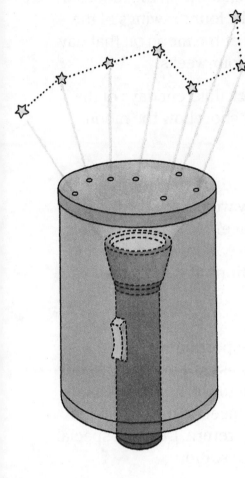

4 Quickly put your cork into the bottle top. Be sure to aim the bottle away from you and anyone else. You don't want the cork to hit anyone or anything.

5 Gently shake the bottle until the gas bubbles from the seltzer and baking soda push the cork out of the bottle and into the air.

STAR MAKER   Learn about several constellations in the night sky. Pick one and find out how it got its name. Use the pattern of your constellation to make your own indoor star show. You will need an oatmeal box, a flashlight, and a large safety pin.

1 Draw your constellation on the bottom of the oatmeal box on the inside (or draw it backwards on the outside of the box). Mark where the stars are in the constellation. Punch holes in the box very carefully to form your constellation.

2 At night or in a darkened room, place the flashlight in the box and shine it on a blank wall or the ceiling.

3 Show your constellation to others. Tell them about your constellation. Put on a star show with friends who have made their own constellation boxes.

More to try: Learn Native American or native Hawaiian legends about the movement of the stars. Share what you learn with your group.

THE NIGHT SKY   Go stargazing with someone who knows the planets and the stars, or have someone help you read a star map. Try to find the North Star, the Big Dipper, the Milky Way, or other constellations. Look for planets and satellites overhead. Perhaps you will even see a meteor or a meteor shower.

More to try: Make up your own constellation while looking at the stars. Tell a story about how it got its name. Help someone else to find it. Use binoculars or a telescope to view the moon and planets.

THE MOON   The moon looks as if it has a changed shape at different times during the month. The moon is not really changing shape; the earth makes a shadow on the moon as they both move through space. Make four drawings of the moon. Pick a day of the week. Look at the moon on that day to make your drawings. Do this for four weeks.

More to try: Do this with friends. Pick different days of the week so you can have pictures that show how the moon changes day by day.

READY, SET, JET!   Pretend that you are on a journey to a Girl Scout center on the moon. How would you dress for space? How would you move in space? Make a drawing of what you would wear on your journey. Show your drawing to others. Be ready to answer questions about your space outfit.

OR

Many Girl Scout events, or "wider opportunities," have special patches to celebrate the occasion. For example, our Girl Scouts who travel to Antarctica to work with scientists give a special patch to people they meet on the trip and to Girl Scouts they speak to when they return. Design a special patch to take to the moon or a space station.

MATH FUN

Jr. Troop 447 did with girls

Did you know that you use math every day? When you count money, or measure your height and weight, or tell time, you are using math. Try these activities to discover more ways to use math and have fun at the same time.

CAN YOU GUESS?   Find out how well your friends and family can guess amounts. Find a large jar with a lid. Fill it with something like seeds, beans, or marbles. Count each one as you fill the jar. Have at least five people guess the number of objects that are in the jar. Ask family and friends to record their guesses and how they made them. Let them pick up the jar if they wish. Did anyone make a close guess? You might want to make an award for the winner.

done

MY NUMBERS   Numbers are used to tell many things about you. For instance, you use numbers to tell how old you are. Think of as many things about yourself that can be described with numbers. Make a "My Numbers" poster that tells all your important numbers facts. Work with friends so you can share ideas.

done

MATH AND ME   Read page 63 in the *Brownie Girl Scout Handbook*. Make a time line about yourself like the one shown.

MEASURE UP   Did you know that many years ago distance was often measured using the size of a human body. For example, a foot was the length of a man's foot. This could cause problems because not everyone had the same size foot.

You can measure things by making up your own system. Choose something to be your unit of measurement, such as a paper clip, an eraser, a pencil, an index card, or your shoe. Then use this unit to measure a table, a chair, the sidewalk, or your room. Measure five things using your system.

More to try: In most countries around the world, the metric system of measurement is used. Find a ruler that has both inches and centimeters and practice measuring using both sides.

WORKING TOGETHER   Read pages 113 and 114 in your *Brownie Girl Scout Handbook* about "Troop Money." Plan a budget for a fun way to earn money for a troop activity.

ALPHABET CODE   Make up your own secret code. Write down the letters of the alphabet. Next to each letter put a different number from 1–26. You don't have to write the numbers in order. Now you have your code. Use your code to write your name in numbers. In place of the letters of your name, write the numbers. You can share your code with friends and send messages using numbers.

More to try: Give a dollar value to each letter of the alphabet. For example, A = $1.00, B = $2.00, C = $3.00, and so on. Then add up the dollars that are in the letters of your first name. You may use pencil and paper or a calculator if you have one. Find the most expensive word or name you can.

43

SCIENCE IN ACTION

Science is a part of our daily life. Science is in action when you use machines, go to the doctor, or grow a plant. Something as basic as bread making involves a complex chemical reaction. Keeping time has advanced through better technology. This Try-It will help you see science in action.

COMPUTER FUN FAIR   Organize or participate in a computer fun fair. Find a computer that you and your friends can use. Have people in your troop bring computer games to a meeting and try them, or visit a store that carries computer games and have an employee give you a demonstration. Decide what to look for in a good computer game.

ENERGY SLEUTH   Think of the kinds of energy that you use daily. Do you use electricity? Do you use gas or oil? Do you use solar energy or thermal power? Keep a record of the times you use some form of energy, other than your own power, for a full day. Look closely at your list. Are there any ways that you can save energy each day? Find at least three ways and try them for a week.

More to try: Create a poster or sign to help family members or friends at school conserve energy in some way.

RAINBOW MAKING   You have probably stopped to look at a beautiful rainbow sometime in your life. Now you can make your own and learn why rainbows happen in the natural world. You will need a clear plastic cup, water, a flashlight, food coloring (red, green, and blue), and a piece of heavy white paper that will stand up when folded in half. You will also need crayons and a ruler. Set up your experiment on a table or counter in a room that can be darkened.

1 Fill your cup with water halfway and place it near the edge of your table. Place the folded paper about three inches behind the glass to make a screen. Be careful not to knock over your water.

2 Turn on your flashlight and turn off the lights. Hold the flashlight against the edge of the table and shine the light up through the water so that the light hits the screen behind the cup. Change the angle so that a band of colors appears on your screen. Copy your color band on another piece of paper and label the colors. What have you created?

3 What happens when you change the angle of the flashlight? What happens if you move the flashlight toward the table or away from the table while still shining the light through the water onto the screen? What is the water doing to the light beam to create your colors?

4 Now let's try something else. Using your food color, put three drops in to change the color of the water to red. Shine the light through the water. Is anything different when you create your color band? Try to guess what would happen if you use blue or green water, and then dump out the red water and make the experiment.

5 Can you guess what you need to have a rainbow in the out-of-doors?

COMPUTERS IN YOUR LIFE   Use a computer at home or at school to solve a problem, check your spelling, write a story, or learn something new.

OR

Talk to three people who use computers at work. Find out what they do and what kind of help and information they get from their computers. Ask them how they learned to use a computer. Tell others what you learned.

TIME CHECK   Read the section on time on pages 110–112 in your *Brownie Girl Scout Handbook*. Do one of the activities on page 111 about time, as well as the following activity. Look around you for different ways of telling time. Find a simple way to tell time, such as with a sundial or a water clock. Compare a grandfather clock or old-fashioned pocket watch to a digital clock or watch. How are they alike? How are they different?

  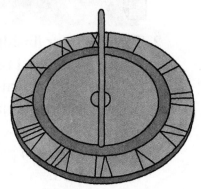 

OR

Read the section on tools on pages 130–131 in your *Brownie Girl Scout Handbook*. Then make something using some tools.

BREAD MAKING   All sorts of things happen when you make a loaf of yeast bread. Yeast is really millions of tiny one-celled plants that start to grow when you add water or milk. Without the yeast, your bread would not have all those wonderful air spaces that make it light and fluffy. Many of the things we cook depend upon the chemistry between ingredients to arrive at the finished product.

46

This is a great activity for a rainy day. Be sure to do it with an adult. You need a kitchen with an oven and the following items:

1 package or cake of yeast
2 cups of lukewarm milk
2 tablespoons of sugar
1 tablespoon of salt
6 cups of flour
5 tablespoons of butter
a large mixing bowl
a wooden spoon
two loaf pans
a small pan for melting butter
a kitchen towel

1 Wash your hands.
2 Place the two cups of lukewarm milk into your bowl. (Warm the milk slightly if it has been in the refrigerator.) Add yeast and sugar and salt. Stir with the wooden spoon so the yeast dissolves.
3 As you add the flour, little by little, stir it with the wooden spoon. When it really becomes hard to mix with the spoon, melt and slowly add the butter. Mix it with the spoon. Continue to add the flour to the mixture until it is all used up. By this time you may want to use your hands (be sure they are clean) to mix the dough.
4 The dough should look smooth and be stretchable. Now you get to knead the dough. This can be done on a wooden breadboard or on your kitchen counter. Fold the dough back upon itself and beat it down for about five to ten minutes. Take turns if you are doing this as a group. When you are finished kneading, shape your dough into a nice big ball and place it in the mixing bowl again. Cover it with a towel and place it in a warm spot in the kitchen.

Now comes the easy part. You have to wait for an hour and a half or two hours for the chemical reaction to take place. You should let the dough grow until it is double its original size. What is happening here? The yeast plants are reacting with the sugar and produce carbon dioxide, which is a gas. When the bread dough is warmed, the carbon dioxide gas bubbles grow larger and cause the dough to rise.

5 After your dough has grown to twice its size, it is time to punch it. What happens when you punch it hard two or three times? Sprinkle some flour on your breadboard or table and take your dough out to knead it for about three to four minutes.

6 Divide your dough into two equal parts. Coat the inside of your loaf pans with butter or vegetable oil. Mold each portion of dough into the shape of the pan and put it in the loaf pan. Cover the loaf pans with your towel in a warm place. The loaves should double in size again.

7 When your loaves are doubled in size, pop them in an oven at a temperature of 375°F. Bake for around 45 minutes or until the loaves are a nice golden brown. Remove the loaves from the oven with a hot pad. Cool the loaves before removing them from the pan. Eat the bread while it is still warm.

When you cut the bread, notice the texture. During the baking, the carbon dioxide bubbles have continued to grow and to create those air spaces. All the better for butter and jam!

MY BODY

Your body is a wonderful living machine. It has many parts that all work together. Try these activities to find out more about your body.

PULSE   Your heart pumps blood through the body. Every time your heart beats, it pushes a new supply of blood into your arteries. You can feel this as your pulse. The blood then goes into your veins and back to your heart.

Take your pulse by placing three fingers on the hand you write with flat on the side of your neck. (See the diagram.) Hold them still until you feel a slight beating. Now try to feel your pulse in your wrist. Hold your fingers as the diagram shows. You can even watch your pulse. Try this. Put a thumbtack through one end of a wooden match. Rest your arm on a table. Rest the thumbtack with the match on the spot on your wrist where you found your pulse. Watch closely. What happens?

More to try: Try to find a different spot on your body where you can feel your pulse. Practice taking someone else's pulse.

BRAIN POWER   Your brain controls your body, from moving and thinking to breathing. It makes certain your body keeps working no matter what you are doing. Your brain has helped you do all the Try-It activities in this book. Try these four activities to see how your brain works.

Different Muscles   Sit at a table and write your name. Then take one of your feet and move it in a circle on the floor. Now try doing both things together. Sometimes it's hard for your brain to do two things at once.

Eye to brain to hand   Cut a piece of paper the size of a dollar bill. Hold it high over your head and then drop it. Try to catch it before it falls on the floor. Sometimes an object falls faster than messages travel from your hand to your arm. Try to improve through practice.

Spinning   In a wide, clear space, stand with your arms straight out and spin around about 10 times. How do you feel when you stop? Your eyes and ears help you balance. When you spin fast, your eyes and ears can't send normal messages to the brain and you feel dizzy.

Dreams   Your brain works even while you're sleeping— that's why you have dreams. In a circle with friends, tell about one of your dreams.

FINGERPRINTS   Your fingerprints are unlike anyone else's. Even identical twins have different fingerprints. Do the fingerprinting activity on page 46 in the *Brownie Girl Scout Handbook*. Then make fingerprints of three other people on clean white paper.

Here is one way to make fingerprints. You will need a soft lead pencil, white paper, and clear tape.

1 On a piece of paper, use the pencil to make a large dark spot about the size of a quarter.
2 On a clean sheet of white paper, trace your hand or the hand of the person who is going to be fingerprinted.
3 Rub a fingertip on the pencil spot.
4 Press the fingertip down on a small piece of clear tape.

5 Put the tape on the fingertip of the hand tracing.
6 Do this with each finger.

Do some look alike? Try this with your family.

REFLEXES   Reflexes are things your body does automatically. There are many kinds of reflexes. Try the following activities to find out about a few. Do these with a friend.

Eye Changes   In a well-lit room, sit facing a friend. Hold a card over one of her eyes. Then quickly pull it away. Watch what happens to the black center part of the eye called the pupil. The colored part of the eye, the iris, is changing with the light. Your body does this automatically.

Knee Jerk   Sit on something that is high enough so that your feet don't touch the floor. Cross your legs. On the top leg, feel your kneecap. Just below your kneecap is a soft spot. Have a friend gently tap this spot with the back of this book.

Muscle Reaction Make one of your arms very straight. Ask a friend to hold your arm down while you try as hard as you can to lift it. Your friend can use both hands. Count to twenty, trying as hard as you can to lift your arm. After you have counted to twenty, your friend can let go. Stand still and let your arm relax. What does your arm do?

More to try: Ask a doctor or nurse to help you learn more about reflexes.

A FIT BODY Make exercise a regular part of your day. Exercise is important to keep your body healthy. Make the fitness wheel on page 55 in the *Brownie Girl Scout Handbook* and then do some of the exercises.

More to try: Before doing an exercise, have a friend count how many times you breathe out in a half minute. Count again after you have finished an exercise. Your lungs are working harder to bring in oxygen as you work out.

BODY PARTS Your body has many parts that work together. Some people may have a disability. Arms or legs or other parts of their bodies may not function normally or at all or may be missing. People with disabilities learn new ways to do things. They may also get help from medicine and special machines or tools.

With one or more friends, make a list of how your bodies are the same. Then make a list of how your bodies are different. Talk with each other about the lists.

More to try: Find out about disabilities. Read pages 80–81 in your *Brownie Girl Scout Handbook.* Here's a simple activity that will show you how a disability can make life more difficult and what a person can do to help herself or himself. All you will need is some tape. Tape your thumbs to the sides of your hands. Now try to open a door or lift a can or write your name. Try to do other things with your thumb taped. Is it hard? Can you get better with practice?

ART TO WEAR

Art can be many different things. It can be a painting or music or a poem. You can even wear works of art.

T-SHIRT MAGIC Turn a plain T-shirt or sweatshirt into your own work of art. Make a simple design or a sketch at a size that will fit onto your T-shirt. When you are satisfied with your design or picture sketch, you are ready to draw or paint on the T-shirt. Use crayons or paint made for painting on cloth. Follow the directions that come with the crayons or paint. Have a fashion show with the shirts you and your troop make.

More to try: Learn to tie-dye, to add buttons and bows to a shirt, or to create a design with iron-on fabric.

OR

Hats can do more than keep your head warm. They can also show what a person does for a living. A police officer's hat looks different from a baseball player's cap. Sometimes people wear hats, like party hats, when they're celebrating. Make a special hat for yourself. Construct your hat out of newspaper, or find an old straw or felt hat at home or in a secondhand store. Decorate it with colored paper, fabric scraps, yarn, sequins, buttons, or natural materials.

FACE PAINT   Many cultures through the ages have used face painting to enhance beauty and to mark special occasions. Have a face-painting party. Make certain an adult is present. Be sure to use makeup and paints that are made just for the face. Try different patterns, designs, and colors. If possible, invite a makeup artist to your troop to demonstrate different kinds of face painting.

PAPIER-MÂCHÉ   This is an easy way to make a new bracelet. You will need a cardboard tube that fits loosely over your wrist, scrap paper to make strips out of, colored tissue paper, and flour and water paste.

   "Papier-mâché" is a light material made from wastepaper and glue that can be easily molded. Mix up a paste, using flour and water until it is thin and runny and without any lumps. To make your papier-mâché, you tear strips of paper and dip them into your paste. Layer the strips around the cardboard tube bracelet you have cut to the width you want. Create an even surface or one with patterns and bumps. Use your fingers to mold and shape. For your final layers, use strips of colored tissue paper. Create patterns or a solid surface or paint your bracelet. Place the bracelet in a warm, dry place. The thicker your bracelet is, the longer it will take to dry.

   You can also make papier-mâché flowers or small animals and wear them as pins or necklaces.

MASK MAKING   Many people around the world make masks for ceremonial occasions, holidays, or dramatic events. Choose a holiday or special event to make a mask for. Use a paper bag to create a new personality. Add bits of paper, yarn, or other materials to a paper bag. You can also draw on the bag with crayons or paint. Or use heavy cardboard as a base to create a mask that you hold to your face by a handle. (Chopsticks make good handles.)

BEADS   Create your own beads that you can use to make jewelry. You will need some toothpicks and the ingredients from the dough recipe on page 170 in your *Brownie Girl Scout Handbook*.

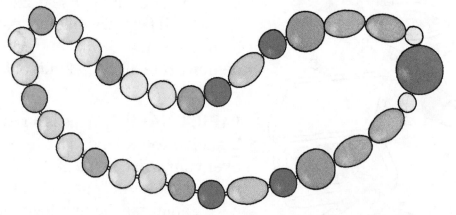

Take pieces of dough about the size of a grape, and roll or press the dough into beads with different sizes and shapes. Use a toothpick to make holes in the beads. Let the beads dry. You can put them on string to make necklaces and bracelets.

More to try: Decorate your beads with colored paints.

KNOTS   You can tie knots to make bracelets, necklaces, belts, and other things. On page 127 in your *Brownie Girl Scout Handbook* are two easy knots to tie. Find different kinds of string, ribbon, ropes, and cords. Look for a variety of colors. Tie square knots until you have the right length. Then tie overhand knots at the end of each piece of rope.

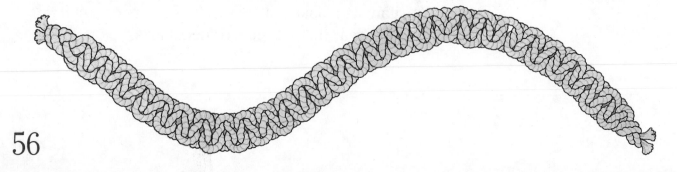

ME AND MY SHADOW

A shadow is formed when a body or object blocks light. Artists study how light falls on things to create shadows, and use this knowledge in their paintings, photographs, and other artwork. You can begin to understand shadows by doing this Try-It.

DOING A SHADOW PLAY   Read "The Brownie Story" on pages 15–22 in your *Brownie Girl Scout Handbook*. With others, act out the play in a shadow theater. You make a shadow theater with a bright light bulb and several old bed sheets. (The picture below should help you to make one.) Act out the play *behind* the sheet while the audience watches the shadows on the front of the sheet.

TRACING YOUR SHADOW With a partner, trace your shadow, either indoors with a bright light bulb shining on you so your shadow falls on the floor or wall, or outdoors on a sunny day. (See the picture.) Take a big piece of paper and tape it on the floor or wall where your shadow falls. Then stay very still while your partner traces your shadow on the paper. Then switch and do your partner's shadow on another piece of paper. Next, using your body, try to make at least six different shadow shapes. Can you make your shadow bigger? smaller? Can you make your shadow a monster? a bird? Can you make your shadow other things?

KEEPING SHADOWS Try this activity with someone who can help you use a camera. Photographers need to understand light, shadows, and shading to compose good photographs. Take some pictures of interesting shadows that you see outdoors. You can use black-and-white film. Notice how things look in light, in shade, and in the dark. Make a display of your photos of interesting shadows.

OR

58

Use studio proof paper to make shadow pictures of small objects. Studio proof paper can be printed without a darkroom or you can use architect's blueprint paper or ammonia paper. Place an object on the shiny side of the special paper in the sunlight. After a few minutes, the paper will turn darker from the sunlight and the paper under the object will stay white. Then "set" your shadow image. Be sure to find out the proper way to set the shadows on the paper you use.

OR

Clean, fresh newspaper will turn dark yellow in bright sunlight. Try to find some that is blank, but regular newspaper is all right. Place a sheet of newsprint in the sun. Lay some objects on top of the paper and leave them for at least a half hour. These shadow designs won't last very long, so show them to others as soon as you can.

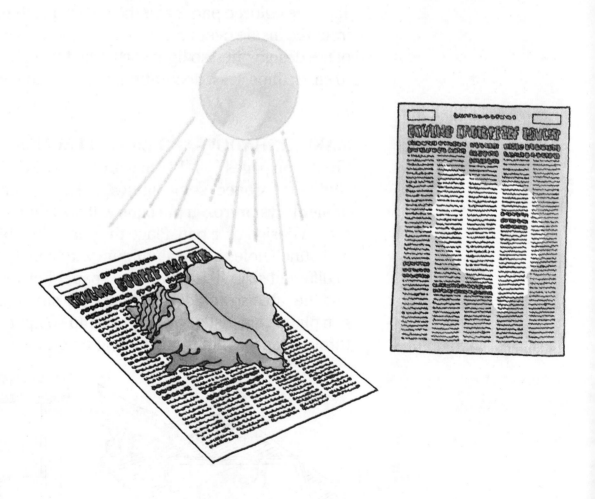

MAKING SHADOW BAGS You'll need a paper shopping bag with handles, scissors, tape or glue, colored construction paper, and colored cellophane paper.

Cut out designs on the sides of your shopping bag. Tape the colored paper and the colored cellophane paper from the inside over parts of your design. Leave some parts of the design open so light can come through. Use the bag to carry things as a decoration, or give it to someone as a gift.

MAKING SHADOW-AND-LIGHT PLAQUES Read about "Tools" on pages 130–131 in your *Brownie Girl Scout Handbook*. Collect some lightweight aluminum pans. (TV dinner trays or frozen pie pans will do.) With a felt marker, draw a design on a pan. Place the pan on a table or counter and punch holes in the aluminum with a hammer and nails of different sizes. Put lots of newspaper between the pan and the table so you don't damage the surface. Place your pan plaque against a window or lamp so light can pass through the nail holes and highlight your design.

MAKING SHADOWY CUTOUTS AND STENCILS Here is a way to make shadowy cutouts and stencils. You will need thin cardboard or thick paper to make the stencils and cutouts, thick poster paint, small sponges, newspapers, and sheets of paper. Then follow these steps:

1 Draw a design on the cardboard or thick paper that is smaller than your sheet-paper size. Push the scissors through the thick paper or cardboard and cut out the design carefully.

2 You should now have a *cutout* (the design you cut out of the cardboard or thick paper) and a *stencil* (the cardboard or paper with the design cut out of it).

3 Place a sheet of clean paper on top of some of the old newspapers. (They will serve as blotters.) Hold the *stencil* down on the paper without moving it. Dip the sponge in the poster paint and dab the paint all through the inside of the stencil. (See the picture.) Remove the stencil and let the paint dry. Take another sheet of paper and put the *cutout* down on it. Without moving the cutout, dip the sponge in the poster paint and dab the paint all around the edge of the cutout. (See the picture.)

CREATIVE COMPOSING

Compose means "to put together," "to make up," "to create." Every person has creative abilities, especially when time is taken to learn about one's self, to listen, to look, to hear, and to do. In this Try-It, you can have fun exploring creative composing.

COMPOSING A SONG   Read about Girl Scout ceremonies on pages 34–36 in your *Brownie Girl Scout Handbook*. Then make up a song for a Girl Scout ceremony. Compose and sing your song with friends.

COMPOSING A POEM   Compose a poem on something you care about—for example, your family, or what you wish for the world. Poems use words in special ways. Sometimes the words rhyme and sometimes they even create a design. Look at the two poems. Follow these examples or try your own ideas. Share your poem with your family and friends.

A RHYMING POEM

We must take care
and be sure to share.
Our world is where we all live.
(Can you think of a line to finish this?)

A WORD PICTURE

Flowers ARE   Happiness
                  Pretty
                  Colors
                  Food
                  Tiny

COMPOSING A MESSAGE Read about sign language on page 81 of your *Brownie Girl Scout Handbook.* Do the two activities in that section. Compose a sign alphabet message with your hands and sign it to someone.

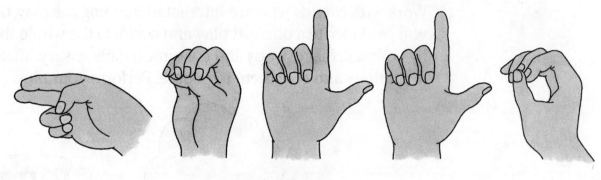

Hello

COMPOSING A PAINTING Think of a special place. It can be a real place that you've seen or a made-up place. First, with a pencil, draw it on a piece of paper. Look at where things are placed in your sketch. Should anything be moved? made smaller? made larger? Then think of colors for your painting. Tempera or water-color paints are best to use. Markers, chalk, crayons, or colored pencils will also do. Show your painting to others.

More to try: Do a small pencil sketch of your painting. Then draw it again on large, heavy white paper.

COMPOSING A PLAY Think about a person or a situation or an event that interests you. Make up a story based on this interest. Then turn the story into a play. Think about who should play the different parts and what they will say. Work with friends who are interested in doing the play, or you could write a one-girl play and perform the whole thing by yourself. Make props and costumes, if necessary. Make invitations and give them to people. Perform your play.

COMPOSING MUSIC FOR INSTRUMENTS Compose a piece of music for professional musical instruments or ones that are homemade. Start an instrumental group and teach your friends to play this composition, or just write and perform a solo. Share the music with others.

OR

Make the melody glasses on pages 173–174 of your *Brownie Girl Scout Handbook.* Try to make up your own songs to play on the glasses.

ARTFUL ARCHITECTURE

An architect is someone who designs buildings and other spaces. You can have fun learning about architecture by doing this Try-It.

YOUR HOME   Read "My Home" on pages 75–76 in the *Brownie Girl Scout Handbook.* Do the three activities on page 75. Then look carefully at the inside and outside of your home. Architects often make designs or drawings of the inside and outside of buildings. Draw a picture of the outside of your home, and, on another piece of paper, draw the inside of your home. Show your pictures to others.

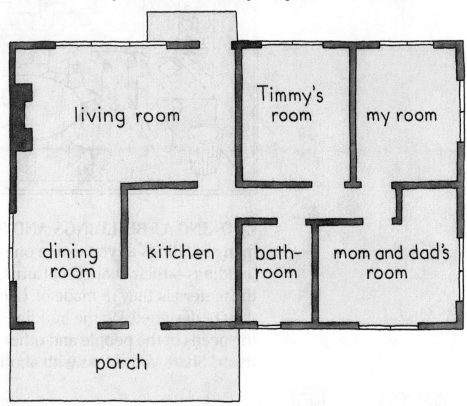

DESIGNING SPACE FOR SOMEONE WITH A DISABILITY   Read about disabilities on page 80 in your *Brownie Girl Scout Handbook.* Think about where you live or where you go to school. What would you change about either of those places to make them safer and more accessible (easy to get at, easy to get around) for someone who is blind? someone who is deaf? someone in a wheelchair? Tell your ideas to another person.

DESIGNING AN IDEAL GIRL SCOUT MEETING PLACE

Think about all the things you do at your Girl Scout meeting place. Then imagine the perfect Girl Scout meeting place. Draw a picture or sketch of it. Using clay, cardboard boxes, paper, wood, or other material, make a model of your ideal Girl Scout meeting place. Show and explain your model to other Girl Scouts. If possible, try out some of your ideas at the meeting place.

LOOKING AT BUILDINGS AND SPACES   Look at as many buildings as you can in one day. Notice the types of buildings—their shapes, patterns, designs, size, colors, and the materials they're made of. Look at play areas and how they're designed. Do the buildings and spaces you see meet the needs of the people and other living things that use them? Share your ideas with another person.

DISCOVERING THE STRENGTHS OF SHAPES

Architects have to know how strong building materials are and what weights different shapes can hold. Experiment with the strengths of designs and shapes by following these steps.

1 Sit on the floor. Take a single sheet of paper. Hold it by one edge in the air so the paper sticks out straight over the floor. Next, take a small stone, coin, or button and place it on the paper. (See the picture.) What happens? (The flat piece of paper should be too thin and flimsy to hold up the stone, coin, or button. It does not have enough strength to support the object.)

2 Next, take that same piece of paper and fold it in quarters like a book. (See the picture.) Try to rest the stone, coin, or button on the edges of the paper. What happens? (By changing the shape of the paper, there is more strength and the paper can hold up the object.)

3 Make the fan shape and the curved shape out of your paper as in the picture and try to balance the objects on the paper. What happens? (They should be able to support the objects.)

4 Experiment with other curved and folded shapes to see which ones can hold up the stone, coin, or button. Make a design sculpture with your shapes. (Glue or tape may help put the shapes together. You can also make slits in the paper and fit the pieces together.)

More to try: Do this with friends. Using only tape, paper, and scissors, make a model of a house, a store, or some other kind of building. Make a bridge, too.

MY IDEAL NEIGHBORHOOD   Think of an ideal neighborhood. Get a piece of cardboard or oak tag at least 36 inches x 24 inches in measurement. Using that as a base, glue or paste cut-out pictures you find in old magazines that could go in your ideal neighborhood. Get crayons, markers, or paint to draw in other parts of your neighborhood that you think should be included. Explain and show your ideal neighborhood to others.

EARTH AND SKY

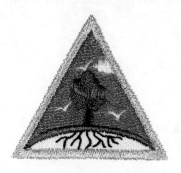

Look down. Look up. What do you see? Earth below and sky above! Discover life in the soil and in the sky.

THE SOIL   Find a special spot in a forested area. Take along a magnifying glass, a spoon or small trowel, a pencil or tweezers, white paper or a plastic dish, and a yard of string.

1 Make a circle with your string on the forest floor. Look on the surface of your circle. What do you find? Do you find plants? any animals? anything else?
2 Next, dig three small holes in your circle to look below the surface of the forest litter. Can you find differences in plants and animals as you dig down 1″, 3″, and 6″? Is there a difference in how the soil feels or in its color as you go deeper? Use your white paper or plastic dish to help you study soil critters as you find them.
3 Share your findings with someone or the group. Carefully fill the holes and leave your circle as you found it.

More to try: Do the same activity in an open meadow or in an unpaved vacant lot. Look at a decaying log in the forest, but do not tear it apart.

GOING, GOING, GONE   On a walk or hike, examine the edge of a stream or a place where the ground is bare and exposed on a hillside or slope. Look for places where soil has been worn down or disappeared. What has caused this? A name for this is *soil erosion.*

Do this activity to find out what causes soil erosion. In the backyard or in a sandbox, build a mound of soil about two feet high or knee-high. Pretend that this is a hill or mountainside in your community. Wet the hill with a watering can or a slow, steady stream of water from a hose.

What happens to your hill? Find a slope that is covered with grass or plants. Water it with your watering can. What happens? Is the result different from what happens on your mountain of soil?

More to try: Look at trails as you walk at camp or a public nature center or a park. What happens when people do not stay on the trails? What do people who make trails do to prevent shortcuts and erosion? Can you find water bars (mounds of dirt that help divert water off a trail), steps, bridges, and culverts on a hike?

THE SKY'S MY HOME!   Find a place outside where you can sit and be a "sky watcher." Observe the types of creatures in the air. Also observe the ways these creatures move. Share with your group or a friend the movements you observe by acting them out. Can you find creatures that flap or beat or flutter their wings, or that glide, soar, dive, and twirl, for example? Can you attach sounds to any of these motions? Ask an adult to help you make a list of all the creatures you saw in the air. You might make a scrapbook and include pictures, drawings, and words that describe each animal.

More to try: Build a feeder for a creature of the sky. Be alert for what comes to visit your feeder.

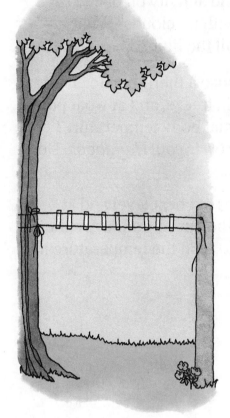

OUR AIR Can you see air? What do you see when skies are gray and there are no clouds? Be an air quality inspector. Here is a way to check the air you breathe for dust and other things that you can see over a period of three weeks. You will need a roll of tape and some string about two-feet long.

1 Find a spot out-of-doors protected from rain and strong winds where you can tie your string. You can use thumbtacks to tack down the ends. (See the illustration.)

2 Each day for three weeks, take a strip of tape about three inches long and write the date on the nonstick side. Put a piece of tape on the string so that the sticky side is on the outside. (See the diagram.) At the end of three weeks, you should have a record of particles from the air. Which tape strip is cleanest? At what day do you start to notice a change? What do you think makes up the particles in the air that you can see? There are a lot of things in the air that are not visible to the naked eye. What do some of these things come from? Can you think of any other ways that you might measure air pollution?

More to try: Have you ever been in a room where adults are smoking cigarettes? How does it make you feel? Find out how smoking hurts your lungs. See if you can help someone you know stop smoking.

CLOUDS   Read about "Clouds and Rain" on page 118 of your *Brownie Girl Scout Handbook.* Do the cloud-watching activity. Be sure to dress for the weather. If it is a warm day, perhaps you can lie on the ground and look up at the clouds. Describe what you see to a friend. Make up a story about your favorite cloud. Perhaps you want to make cloud pictures as described in the second activity on page 118. What would it be like in a world with no clouds? What would it be like if it were cloudy all the time?

HOT AND COLD   Learn how to use a thermometer. Find out at what temperature water will freeze, and at what point water will boil? What is your normal body temperature? Turn to page 116 in your *Brownie Girl Scout Handbook.* Do the activities in the "Sun" section.

More to try: Measure temperatures at chest level and at ground level in different parts of the out-of-doors. Are there differences? Use a thermometer to read the temperature in the sun and shade.

WATER EVERYWHERE

Water is important to everyone. We use it for drinking, for cleaning, for transportation, for fun. We depend upon it for our crops and dam it in rivers for energy. But people are not the only creatures to use water. What happens if it does not rain, or people pollute the water? Can you find out about water *without* getting wet?

DRIP DROP   Read "Be a Water and Energy Saver" on pages 83–84 in the *Brownie Girl Scout Handbook*. Do the suggested activities and also find a faucet that leaks around your house, school, camp, or neighborhood park. Put a measure under it and time how long it takes to fill up. How many cups or even gallons are wasted in a day at this site? See if you can get someone to fix the faucet or learn how to fix it with someone who knows how to make the repair.

CLEAN, CLEAR WATER   Do a taste test using water from the tap, distilled water, and bottled spring water. Can you taste a difference? Where does the tap water come from in your home, at your school, and at your camp?

Try this, BUT NO TASTE TESTS!

1 Do some simple tests using coffee filters and a funnel. Gather some water samples from mud puddles, standing water, a lake or a stream, the tap, and other sources.
2 Write in pencil on the edge of each filter the name of your water source. Strain that water through the filter.
3 Compare filter papers. Is there a difference between any of them?

Many of the harmful substances found in water are smaller than the holes in your filter paper. These must be taken out of the water by a better filter system or killed by boiling or by use of certain chemicals. How do you know when water is safe to drink?

WATER SNOOPER Construct a water snooper. Have someone help you remove both ends of a large can. Take some clear plastic wrap and put it on one end of the can. Hold it in place with rubber bands. You can use this snooper to look into a pond or tide pool, or an aquarium or puddle, by submerging the end with the plastic into your water.

More to try: Make a water-drop magnifying lens. Take a piece of clear plastic wrap and put two or three drops of water in the middle of it. Hold the plastic over the letters in this book. Are they larger? Hold the plastic over other objects.

Now try to make this special viewing box. Take a milk or juice carton and cut the top off. Cut a hole in the side of the carton. Make the hole about the size of a grape. Stretch plastic wrap tight across the top, and hold it there with a big rubber band. Place an object in the bottom of the carton through your side hole. Place a drop of water on top of the plastic wrap and look through it. Your object should look larger than life.

WATER EXPLORER   Visit a pond, lake, small stream, or a protected tide pool with your troop or with an organized group. Look for creatures and plants that live in the water. Dip a strainer in the water and empty what you find in a white plastic bowl. If you find living things, how do they move? Look under rocks in the water. Do they hide under them or cling to them? Remember to leave the area as you found it. Use the water snooper to see into the water.

More to try: Visit an aquarium. Create an aquarium with pond water and draw the changes that take place over a period of time.

MADE OF WATER   Water is part of more things than you may think. For example, your body is made up of water more than anything else. Water mixes with other things so that it often doesn't look like water—milk and orange juice are two examples. Try to find food containers that list water as an ingredient. Work with friends.

More to try: Find foods that you make by adding water. Plan a refreshment break with these foods. Notice the changes in these foods before and after you have prepared them.

BUBBLE MAKERS   Water can do some strange things when mixed with other ingredients. Try this activity outdoors.

1 Make your own bubble mix with liquid dishwashing soap (1 part), water (1 part), and glycerine (1 part). Glycerine is a liquid that can be purchased at a drugstore.
2 Prepare your bubble makers. You can use taped-together soda straws, plastic lids cut out and held with clothespins, bent wire, or plastic thread spools.

Bubbles survive longer when it is a humid or rainy day. Can you guess why? Who can make the biggest bubble? the most interesting? the longest?

75

OUTDOOR ADVENTURER

Doing activities outside is a special part of being a Brownie Girl Scout. Walking, hiking, and camping out require special knowledge and skills. Before doing any of the activities below, review the outdoor skills checklist on page 122 in your *Brownie Girl Scout Handbook*.

NEIGHBORHOOD MAP   Pretend that you are a bird looking down on the earth. Draw a map of your meeting place, backyard, or a neighborhood park as you might see it from above. Put in buildings, pathways, vegetation, and other things of interest.

1   Make a map key on a lower corner of your map. A map key uses symbols or colors to represent things that you put on your map. For example, a star-shaped symbol may represent a tree, or the color blue may represent water.

2   Try out your map on a buddy. Hide a colored piece of paper somewhere in the area represented by your map. Place an "X" on your map to mark the hiding place. Give the map to your buddy and see if she can find the hidden paper.

WEATHER   Do the dress-for-the-weather relay activity on page 61 of your *Brownie Girl Scout Handbook*.

POCKETKNIFE   Learn to use a pocketknife by following the instructions in the *Brownie Girl Scout Handbook* on pages 127–128. Practice opening and closing a pocketknife, passing a knife to someone, and using the knife. Try to skin and cut a carrot into sticks for an outdoor snack.

A HIKE   Plan a day hike in a forest, park, or nature preserve. Include clothing, a snack or sack lunch, and safety measures in your plan. Use a map of the area when making your plan. Do one of the activities in "Move Out" on pages 124–125 in your *Brownie Girl Scout Handbook* or one of the following:

1 Try following a nature trail that leads you on a guided exploration of the area.

2 Try a color hike. Take a box of colored crayons with you on your hike with at least one color for each person. Try to find things that match the crayon colors.

3 Try a nature-sounds scavenger hunt. You will need a portable tape recorder for this. Try to find the following sounds and record them on your nature hike: running water, a buzzing insect, a bird chirp, an alarm sounded by an animal, leaves crunching, wind whistling, something clanking, something pounding, something falling.

CAMP Visit your council camp or day-camp area before the camping season starts and do one of the following activities:

1 Try a unit tour. Using a map of the camp, find out where the girls stay overnight or where the activities are held. If possible, have an older Girl Scout show you about.
2 Try a special hike or activity that you haven't done before from "A Hike." (See pages 76–77.)
3 Learn a camp song that you can sing on your visit.

SLEEP OUT! Plan for and go on an overnight with your troop in someone's backyard, a troop camping facility, or a council camping-out area. Review your outdoor skills. Plan a well-balanced menu that is easy to prepare. Include some "no-cook" items that you can eat while hiking and also at meal times. Make a kaper chart for your group to include individual responsibilities, such as meal fixers, table setters, dishwashers, and cleanup crew. Try some special Brownie Girl Scout activities such as:

1 A Try-It activity from the World of the Arts or the World of the Out-of-Doors.
2 An evening campfire or a puppet show about outdoor wildlife.
3 Making s'mores and singing Brownie Girl Scout songs.

EARTH IS OUR HOME

Everything we do affects our environment in one way or another. You, and all other people, and plants and animals share the earth together. You help take care of the earth and all the living creatures on it. Explore some ways to understand our home, the earth, and help make it a better place.

MINI-ENVIRONMENT STUDY   Do the "Mini-Environment Study" activity on page 83 in your *Brownie Girl Scout Handbook*.

More to try: Using toothpicks, Popsicle sticks, or twigs, mark some points of interest in your "mini-environment" and create a mininature trail. Take a friend along your trail, explaining the special places you have chosen to mark.

RECIPE FOR A MINIWORLD   A terrarium is a small world in an enclosure and is made up of living things, soil, water, and air. It is surrounded by a covering that lets in light. The earth we live on is covered by air and is like a huge terrarium. Plants and animals need soil, air, water, and light in order to survive in both a terrarium and on the earth. If any of these things are lacking or unbalanced by pollution, the plants and animals will suffer.

Have someone help you make your own healthy terrarium. Here are some things to use:

- A clear widemouthed jar (like a peanut butter jar)
- 2 handfuls of small rocks or sand
- 2 handfuls of soil
- 1 handful of dead leaves
- some moss from a forest, a vacant lot, or elsewhere
- several small ferns or plants from a forest, a vacant lot, or a plant store. (Do not pick protected plants or overpick an area. Ask permission to gather materials if you are not on your own property.)

Follow these steps to make your terrarium:

1 Put the sand in first, then the soil, and layer them evenly. Place the dead leaves on top.
2 Using a pencil, tongs, or a chopstick, make holes and plant your plants. Use the moss to fill in around the plants after you have tapped the soil down gently.
3 Water your world with a squeeze bottle or sprinkle water with your hands, but do not drench your world.
4 Place the lid on your jar. Keep the lid closed, as your world should have everything it needs to survive. Place the jar in good light, but not directly in the sunlight.

Observe your terrarium daily. You might want to keep a diary of what you see or make some sketches. Watch for changes. Are there any new plants or animals? What happens if you remove your terrarium from light? What happens if you place it in direct sunlight?

More to try: Make a large terrarium with friends in your troop.

TREES ARE IMPORTANT Trees are so important to our world. They are nice to look at, they provide shelter and homes for animals and people, they provide shade, they provide food and many other things. But most important of all, trees provide oxygen, or the air we breathe. All green plants breathe in carbon dioxide, a gas that we breathe out, and breathe out oxygen, a gas that we breathe in. Trees also help fight air pollution by removing some of the pollutants as they breathe. They help with noise pollution, too.

Plant a tree. It could be on Arbor Day or Earth Day, or maybe even your birthday. Care for it until it is big enough to care for itself, or make sure to plant it in an area where it will take root and grow by itself. Or participate in a tree planting that is part of a reforesting of an area on public lands.

More to try: Read the Dr. Seuss book called *The Lorax*. (Your school library or a public library may have a copy.) Discuss how the Lorax works to save the last trufula tree from the axes of the Thneeds. Your troop might want to read this book as a group and act out the story.

HOW LONG DOES IT TAKE? Collect a sample of trash and garbage to create your own landfill. Include plastic, glass, aluminum, fast-food containers, soda straws, plant clippings, grass, an apple core, some orange rind, a stick of gum, a candy wrapper, and some newspaper.

1 Put the trash into a nylon stocking. Make a list and a drawing of what goes into the stocking as a record.
2 Bury the stocking completely in the earth and mark the location.
3 Wait 2–3 months. Dig up the stocking and the trash. What do you discover? Be sure to wear gloves and avoid touching items in your landfill. You might use a stick or a small trowel to look at the items in your stocking. Have any of the items changed? How have they changed? Are there some things in your stocking that will keep a lifetime? What happens to garbage that leaves your house? Does it get buried like your stocking? Is any of it recycled? Does it get hauled to a dump far away from your town?

More to try: Keep track of how many bags of trash your family sends to the dump in a month.

RECYCLING   Read about being a recycler on page 84 of your *Brownie Girl Scout Handbook*. Then recycle something. You may live in a community where your family is already recycling things because of a recycling law or by choice. Cans, newspapers, and glass are the most frequently recycled items. Check in your community and see how paper boxes and oil are recycled.

1 If your family does not recycle, find out what you can recycle and work out a recycling system with your family.
2 Recycle a toy or a game or a doll by giving it away or giving it to an organization that will fix it and give it to other children.
3 Recycle an article of clothing by passing it on to someone in your family or to an organization that offers clothing to the needy.
4 Recycle by making something useful out of something that is no longer used.

TRASH BUSTERS   Participate in a litter pickup or a community cleanup day.

More to try: Adopt a park or a special place for a troop year. Keep it clean and help educate others to keep it clean as well. Participate in a "Keep America Beautiful" project. Help your parents and family develop better antilitter habits.